HOW TO
WIN
AT THE SPORT OF
BUSINESS

HOW TO WIN

AT THE SPORT OF
BUSINESS

IF I CAN DO IT,
YOU CAN DO IT.

MARK CUBAN

DIVERSION
BOOKS

Diversion Books
A Division of Diversion Publishing Corp.
www.DiversionBooks.com

For more information, email info@diversionbooks.com

Paperback ISBN: 978-1-6357685-9-6
eBook ISBN: 978-0-9839885-3-3

Printed in the United States of America
10 9 8 7 6 5 4 3 2 1

CONTENTS

INTRODUCTION

I can't tell you how many times I have been asked to write a book. More times than I can recall. The reality is that I don't want to write a book. Why not? Because I'm not done yet! I'm young. I'm fun. I'm marginally ugly and I have a great family. I'm just beginning to get good. It is too early to write a book.

What I have written, however, are blog posts. Lots of them. Most of them are about starting businesses. Many are about the challenges entrepreneurs face. Some are about what is involved in running a business. Others are about life in general.

So rather than write a book, I decided to aggregate, curate (see how I used current buzzwords right there?) and update some of my more popular and personal blog posts from the past seven years.

As you go through this collection, don't feel you have to read it like a book. Use it as a way to get fired up. A way to get motivated. Something you can go back to when you need it. Scan it and find the posts that you can relate to. Or read every single word of every post. Either way, I hope you will find a nugget or three that will help you to reach your goals and have more fun in your life.

If there is an overriding theme, it is my wish for you to recognize that if I can become the luckiest person in the world, then with a little bit of work, and yes some luck, you can give me a run for my money for the title. I won't relinquish it easily, but you can be certain I will love the competition!

Love it or hate it, when you are done, find me on Cyber Dust under **+MCuban** to let me know what you think. I can't promise I will respond to you, but your chances of a response will certainly improve if you tell me how brilliant you found all of this and, more importantly, how you convinced all of your friends and coworkers to buy copies as well. Hey, I never said I was subtle!

PART ONE: THE DREAM

I did it too. I would drive by big houses and wonder who lived there—every weekend I would do it. What did they do for a living? How did they make their money? Someday, I would tell myself, I would live in a house like that. I read books about successful people. In fact, I read every book or magazine I could get my hands on. I would tell myself that one good idea would pay for the book and could make the difference between me making it or not. *(And hopefully this book will make the difference for you!)*

I worked jobs I didn't like. I worked jobs I loved but that had no chance of becoming a career. I worked jobs that barely paid the rent. I had so many jobs my parents wondered if I would ever be stable. Most of them aren't on my résumé anymore because I was there so short a time or they were so stupid I was embarrassed. You don't want to write about selling powdered milk or selling franchises for TV repair shops.

In every job, I would justify it in my mind, whether I loved it or hated it, that I was getting paid to learn and every experience would be of value when I figured out what I wanted to do when I grew up.

If I ever grew up, I hoped to run my own business. It's exactly what I told myself every day. In reality, I had as much doubt as confidence. I was just hoping the confidence would win over the doubt and it would all work out for the best.

We all want our dream job or to run our own companies. The truth? It's a lot easier said than done. We need jobs that pay the bills, and we can't wait out the search for the perfect situation. Which leads to the question: What kind of job should you settle for when you can't or don't have the job you want?

Not everyone's situation is going to be the same, but for the recent graduate, or if you find yourself in a job you don't like, or if you are unemployed, the answer is pretty straightforward (at least I thought it was when I graduated college). You continue your education.

Go back to school? No. Get your MBA? No.

For most recent college grads, you just spent the last four or so years paying tuition to get an education. Now that you have graduated, it's your chance to get paid to learn. And what if you aren't a recent college grad? *The same logic applies. It is time to get paid to learn.*

When I graduated from Indiana University, I certainly didn't dream of working for a bank. I wanted a job where I could learn more about computers. So I took a job working for Mellon Bank in Pittsburgh. I helped on systems conversions. Taking old manual systems at small banks and helping them convert to automated systems. I wasn't that good at it. The job was fun for the first couple months because I worked with a lot of fun people. A lot of fun people that liked to hang out and drink after work.

But as the months wore on, I liked it less and less, and I had to remind myself, more and more, exactly why I was there. I was getting paid to learn about how computers work, how big companies work and how middle managers work—that was a whole lot better than paying tuition to get a business education.

I lasted all of nine months at that job. I lasted about eight months at my next job, working for a company called Tronics 2000. At Tronics 2000, our mission was to try franchise the TV repair industry. The company was supposed to be entrepreneurial. It was supposed to be looking into franchising the computer repair business as well. (They had me write an analysis of the opportunity in my off-time). As it turns out, it basically was none of the above. But I got paid my $1500 per month and I learned a whole lot.

The company sold a total of one franchise. Which *I* sold. Again, I was far from a great employee. I spent too much time having fun at the expense of doing my job to the best of my ability. Going to work hung over once a week isn't a good career move. So, in some respects I cheated them. No excuses on my part.

The job was also frustrating. Calling and calling and calling on TV repair shops trying to explain the value of franchising wasn't easy. But I learned how to cold-call. I learned not to be afraid of going through the phone book and making calls.

I also got to talk to an old industry veteran, Larry Menaugh. Larry wrote the very first service contracts in the *television* industry. He was a wise old vet. We didn't talk much about the company or the industry, but after meetings we would talk about how to get the job done. He would give me honest critiques of things I was doing, and coming from Larry, I knew they were right. I wish I could go back and thank him. I tried to look him up a few years ago, but couldn't find him. If you read this Larry, thank you.

As I said, I lasted in that job about nine months, and from there took off to Dallas, Texas, in search of fun, sun, money and women.

I was 23. I had no money. The '77 Fiat I was driving drank oil faster than I could drink beer and had a huge hole in the floorboard. I was going to stay on the floor of some friends who had moved from IU to a huge apartment complex called The Village in Dallas.

I had no idea what the future would bring. I was unemployed and heading to Dallas with zero job prospects. But I knew I had taken a few classes in real-world business and got paid for it instead of paying tuition, and I had every intention of continuing to do the same thing until things worked out. When I got to Dallas, I drove up to the address my friend Greg Schipper had given me. I don't think he expected me to move in. It wasn't like I had many living options. In fact, since he was the only person I knew in town, crashing at his apartment was my only option.

Shippy lived in a three-bedroom apartment with four other friends in Dallas. I became roommate number six. This wasn't a really nice place we all kicked in to move up for. This place has since been torn down—probably condemned. I didn't have my own bedroom. I slept on the couch or floor, depending on what time I got home. I had no closet. Instead, I had a pile that everyone knew was mine. My car still had the its hole in the floorboard and that '77 Fiat X1/9 continued to burn a quart of oil that I couldn't afford, week after week.

To make matters worse, because I was living on happy hour food. Any bar that offered free food in exchange for buying 2 beers was my favorite nightly dining establishment. It was cheap in dollars, but heavy in calories. You know all the jokes about the fat kid at the buffet? That was me. I probably gained 30 pounds in a year.

My confidence wasn't exactly at an all-time high, but I was having fun. Don't get me wrong—I truly was having a blast. Great friends, great city, great energy, pretty girls. OK, the pretty girls had no interest in my fat and growing ass at the time, but that's another story …

I was motivated to do something I loved, I just wasn't sure what it was. I made a list of all the different jobs I would love to do. (I still have it.) The problem was that I wasn't qualified for any of them. But I needed to pay the bills.

I finally got a job working as a bartender at a club. It

was a start, but it wasn't a career. I had to keep on looking during the day.

About a week later I answered a want ad in the newspaper for someone to sell PC software at the first software retail store in Dallas. The ad was actually placed by an employment agency. The fee was to be paid by the company, so I gave it a shot.

I put on my interview face and, of course, my interview suit, which just happened to be one of the two polyester suits that I had bought for a grand total of $99. Thank God for "two-fer, two-fer, two-fer Madness" at the local men's clothing store. Gray pinstripe. Blue pinstripe. Didn't matter if it rained, those drops just rolled down the back of those suits. I could crumple them, they bounced right back. Polyester—the miracle fabric.

I wish I could say the blue suit and my interview skills impressed the employment agency enough to set up the interview with the software store. In reality, not many had applied for the job and the agency wanted the fee so they would have sent anyone over to interview. I didn't care.

I pulled out the gray suit for my interview at Your Business Software. I was fired up. It was my shot to get into the computer business, one of the industries I had put on my list! I remember the interview well. Michael Humecki, the Prez, and Doug (don't remember his last name), his partner, double-teamed me. Michael did most of the talking to start. He asked me if I had used PC software before. My total PC experience at the time was on the long forgotten TI-99A that had cost me $79. I used it to try to teach myself BASIC while recovering from hangovers and sleeping on the floor while my roommates were at work. Michael and Doug weren't impressed.

I was pulling out every interview trick I knew. I went through the spiel about how I was a good salesperson (you know, the part of the interview where you are basically begging for a job), using code phrases like "I care about the customer," "I promise to work really, really hard" and "I will do whatever it takes to be successful." Unfortunately, I was getting that *Well, if no one else applies for the job, then maybe* look from Michael.

Finally, Doug spoke up. He asked me, "What do you do if a customer has a question about a software package and you don't know the answer?" All of the possible answers raced through my mind. I had to ask myself if this was the "honesty test question"—you know, where they want to see if you will admit to things you don't know. Is this some trick technology question and there is an answer everyone but me knows? After who knows how long, I blurted out, "I would look it up in the manual and find the answer for them." Ding, ding, ding … Doug just *loved* this answer.

Michael wasn't as convinced, but he then asked me the question I was dying to hear: "Would you not go back to the employment agency at all, so when we hire you we don't have to pay the fee?" I was in.

So my career in Dallas begins. I'm a software salesperson with Your Business Software in Dallas. At $18,000 per year. The first retail software store in Dallas.

I have to sweep the floor and be there to open the store, but that's not a bad thing. When I tell my future ex-girlfriends that I sell software and am in the computer biz, I'm not going to mention the sweeping the floor part.

Plus, I had to wear a suit to work, and the two-fer Madness specials looked good at happy hour after work. At least I thought they looked good after a few beers. Better yet, the store didn't open till 9:30 a.m., which meant if I had a fun night, I had at least a little time to sleep.

I bet right about now you are questioning where my focus was. Where was my commitment to being the future owner of the Dallas Mavericks? Please. I was stoked I had a good job. I was stoked it was in an industry that could turn into a career. At 23, I was just as stoked that the office was close to where the best happy hours were and that I might finally have more than twenty bucks to spend for a night on the town.

Since I'm talking about partying, I do have to say that my friends and I were very efficient in that area. Beyond living off bar food and happy hours, we literally would agree that none of us would bring more than twenty bucks for a weekend night out. This way we all could pace each other. At least that was the way it was supposed to work, and it did until we figured out the key to having a great night out on the cheap. The key was buying a bottle of cheap, cheap champagne. Freixenet Champagne. It was a full bottle, and it cost twelve bucks. (And for those of you who are keeping score, you can go online and buy one today for less than $10!)

Tear the label off and as far as anyone knew it was Dom. Each of us would grab one and sip on it all night. It was far cheaper than repeatedly buying beers or mixed drinks, and we never had to buy a drink for a girl, we just gave them some champagne! Of course the next day was hell, but since when was I responsible enough to care about a hangover?

But I digress. Back to business. As fired up as I was about the job, I was scared. Why? Because I *have* never worked with an IBM PC in my life. Not a single time, and I'm going to be selling software for it. So what do I do? I do what everyone does—I rationalize. I tell myself that the people walking in the door know as little as I do, so if I just started doing what I told my boss I would do—read the manuals—I would be ahead of the curve. That's what I did. Every night I would take home a different software manual, and I would read it. Of course the reading was captivating. Peachtree Accounting. Wordstar, Harvard Graphics, PFS, dBASE, Lotus, Accpac ... I couldn't put them down. Every night I would read some after getting home, no matter how late.

It was easy on the weekends. After drinking that cheap champagne, I wasn't getting out of bed till about 9 p.m., so I had tons of time to lie on the floor and read. It worked. Turns out not a lot of people ever bothered to RTFM (read the frickin' manual), so people started really thinking I knew my stuff. As more people came in, I could offer honest comparisons because I knew all the different software packages we offered, and customers respected that.

Within about six months, I was building a clientele, and because I had also spent time on the store's computers learning how to install, configure and run the software, I started having customers ask me to install the software at their offices. That meant I got to charge for consulting help. Twenty-five bucks an hour that I split with the store. That turned into a couple hundred extra bucks per month and growing. I was raking it in, enough that I could move from The Hill Hotel (that was what we called our apartment) where the six of us lived, into a three-bedroom apartment across the street, where instead of six of us, there were only *three*. Finally, my own bedroom! To make it even more special, I bought my buddy Mike Ochstein's waterbed. Hey, it was the 80s.

I was earning consulting fees. I was getting referrals. I was on the phone cold-calling companies to get new business. I even worked out a deal with a local consultant who paid me referral fees, which led to getting a $1500 check. It was the first time in my adult life that I had more than one thousand dollars to my name.

That was a special moment, believe or not, and what did I do to celebrate? Nope ... I didn't buy better champagne. I had these old ratty towels that had holes in them and could stand on their own in the corner. They were so nasty I needed a shower from drying off after a shower, so I went out and bought six of the fluffiest, plushest towels I could find. I was moving on up in the world. I had the towels. Life was good. Business was good and getting better for me. I was building my customer base, really starting to understand all the technology and really establishing myself as someone who understood the software. More importantly, no, *most* importantly, I realized that I loved working with PCs and technology. I had never done it before. I didn't know when I took the job if this was going to be a job that worked for me or that I would even like, and it turns out I was lucky. I loved what I was doing. I was rolling so well, I was even partying less ... during the week.

Then one day, about nine months into my career as

a salesperson/consultant, I had a prospect ask if I could come to his office to close a deal. Nine in the morning. No problem to me. Problem to my boss, Michael Humecki. Michael didn't want me to go. I had to open the store. That was my job. We were a retail store, not an outbound sales company. It sounded stupid to me back then, too, particularly since I had gone on outbound calls during the day many times before. I guess he thought I was at lunch.

Decision time. It's always the little decisions that have the biggest impact. We all have to make that "make or break" call to follow orders or do what you know is right. I followed my first instinct: Close the sale. I guess I could have rescheduled the appointment, but I rationalized that you never turn your back on a closed deal. So I called one of my coworkers, Barbara Depew to come in and open up the store, I went to the client's office and closed the deal. Next day I came in to Your Business Software, smile on face, check-in-hand from a new customer, and Michael fired me.

Fired. Not the first time it's happened, but it reinforced what I already knew: I'm a terrible employee. I just had to face facts and move on. Rather than getting back on that "How the hell am I going to find a job?" train, the only right thing to do was to start my own company.

My first act of business? Pile into my buddy and former roommate Greg Schipper's 1982 Celica, nicknamed Celly, and drive to Galveston to party. Of course we stayed in only the finest $19.95-a-night, plug-the-hair-dryer-in-the-wall-and-the-circuit-blows motel. Nothing but the best as I prepared for my journey into entrepreneurial territory again. I could say I was preoccupied with how to get my new business off the ground, that while my friends got drunk, did stupid tourist tricks and ate at greasy spoons, I sat by the pool on the one chaise longue chair with rust on the clean side and wrote up my business plan. I didn't. I got just as drunk and ate the same disgusting food. Then we faced the road-trip terror that everyone knows exists, but refuses to admit—the ride home. It wasn't until we pulled up to the apartment that it hit me. No job. No money. No way to pay the bills. But I did have nice towels.

Fortunately the hangover didn't last too long, and I realized I had to get off my ass and make something happen. First day, first task: Come up with a name. This was the start of the microcomputer revolution, and I wanted a name that said what the company was going to do, which was sell personal computers and software and help companies and individuals install them. I was going to offer microcomputer solutions. So, after struggling with different names for about thirty minutes, I chose MicroSolutions, Inc.

Now came the hard part. I had to call all the people I had done business with at my last company and let them know that I had been shitcanned, then ask them if they would come do business with me at MicroSolutions. I got the expected questions. No, I didn't have an office. No, I didn't have a phone yet (other than my home phone). Yes, it was just me. No, I didn't have any investors. The only question I dreaded was whether I had a computer to work with. I didn't. Fortunately, no one asked.

I made a lot of calls and got some decent responses. "We love you, Mark; we want to give you a chance." A lot of "Let's stay in touch." I got two real bites. One from a company called Architectural Lighting and the other from a company called Hytec Data Systems.

Architectural Lighting was looking for a time and billing accounting system to allow them to track their work with clients. I don't remember the name of the software package I told them about (I think it was Peachtree Accounting), but after going out to meet with them it came down to this: I offered to refund 100 percent of their money if the software didn't work for them, and I wouldn't charge them for my time for installing and helping them. In return, they would put up the five hundred bucks it would take for me to buy the software from the publisher, and I could use them as a reference. This was my "no money down" approach to start a business. They said yes. I had a business.

My second call was to Hytec Data, run by Martin Woodall. I met with Martin at the S&D Oyster House on a beautiful June day, and I remember sitting there and him telling me, "I graduated in Computer Science from West Virginia University. I have $50K in the bank and I drive a brand new Cadillac. I know technology better than you. We can work together." I had a customer, and now with Martin's help, I had some hope. Hytec Data sold multi-user systems. The old kind that used dumb terminals. He bundled it with accounting software, and he and a contractor named Kevin would make modifications to the COBOL source code. They were the hardcore geeks who could help me when I needed it. I was still just ten months from my first introduction to PCs, and had no clue about multi-user systems. If I came across prospects that could use their system and software, I would get referrals. That was good.

Even better was Martin's offer of office space. He and Kevin shared office space with the distributor of the computer systems he sold. They had one office that when the son of the CEO of the distributor wasn't using it to study his Spanish, I could use to make calls, and to keep my folders and paperwork in. Still no computer, but hey, I had an office and phone. I was bona fide ...

At some point I'm going to have to go back and look at my appointment books that I kept from those days to remind myself of who my second and third customers were. They were small companies that I got to know very well. They were people that took me under their wing and trusted me, not because I was the most knowledgeable about computers, but because they knew I would do whatever it took to get the job done. People trusted me with keys to their offices. They would find me there when they arrived in the morning, and I was there when they left. I made $15,000 that first year. I loved every minute of it. As time went on my customer base grew. I got my friend and former roommate Scott Susens to help with computer and printer deliveries. Scott was working as a waiter at a steakhouse at the time. I remember asking him over and over if he would help me out. I had a customer that bought a bunch of Epson dot matrix printers from me, and I had to sell Scott on how it wouldn't be hard to learn how to hook a parallel cable to a PC and printer, and how learning all of this would be a career move compared to working at the steakhouse.

Unfortunately, I couldn't pay him as much as the steakhouse. My good fortune was that Scott worked nights and weekends and decided to take some time in the afternoons to help me. Not long after that, he was working full time installing PCs, learning whatever he had to before an installation. It took a while, but he was eventually earning more than he did at the steakhouse. As it turned out, Scott and I worked together not only at MicroSolutions, but he came to work for me at AudioNet/Broadcast.com as well.

Martin also began to play a larger and larger role. His company was growing, and he was watching my company grow. I would get the PC-based stuff; he would get the accounting system stuff. It was a nice split. The better part of the relationship was based on Martin being the most anal-retentive person I had ever met in my life. While I covered my mistakes by throwing time and effort at the problem, Martin was so detail-oriented, he had to make sure things were perfect so there would never be any problems. We could drive each other crazy. He would give me incredible amounts of shit about how sloppy I was. I would give him the same amount back because he was so anal he was missing huge opportunities. We complemented each other perfectly. It would only be a matter of time before we both knew we had to be partners and work together instead of separately.

That first year in business was incredible. I remember sitting in that little office till 10 p.m. and still being so pumped up, I would drive over to the gym I belonged to and run five to ten miles on the treadmill, going through that day and the next in my head. Other days I would get so involved with learning a new piece of software that I would forget to eat and look up at the clock thinking it was 6 or 7 in the evening and realize that it was actually 1 or 2 in the morning. Time would fly by.

It's crazy the things that you remember. I remember my accounts receivable reaching $15K and me telling all my friends. I remember reading the PC DOS manual (I really did) and being proud that I could figure out how to set up startup menus for my customers. I remember going to every single retail store in town—BusinessLand, NYNEX, ComputerLand, CompuShop, all these companies that are long gone—and introducing myself to every salesperson to try to get leads. I would call every big computer company that did anything at all with small businesses: IBM, Wang, Dec, Xerox, Data General, Hewlett Packard, DataPoint (remember them?). I'd set meetings, ask to come to their offices since I couldn't afford to take them to lunch. I didn't need a lot of customers, but my business grew and grew. Not too fast, but fast enough that by the time MicroSolutions had been in business about two years, I had $85K in the bank, a receptionist/secretary, Scott helping me out, and a four-room office that I moved into along with Martin and Hytec Data Systems.

Then I learned a very valuable lesson. Martin had done a great job of setting up our accounting software and systems. I got monthly P&L statements. I got weekly journals of everything coming in and everything going out, payables and receivables. We had a very conservative process where Martin would check the payables, authorize them and then use the software to cut the checks. I would then go through the list, sign the checks and give them to Renee, our secretary/receptionist, to put in envelopes and mail to our vendors.

One day, Martin comes back from Republic Bank, where we had our account. He had just gone through the drive-through and one of the tellers, whom he would see every day when dropping off our deposits, asked him to wait a second. She came back and showed him a check that had the payee of a vendor WHITED OUT and "Renee Hardy," our secretary's name, typed over it. Turns out that in the course of a couple days our secretary had pulled this same trick on $83K of our $85K in the bank. When Martin delivered the news, I was obviously pissed. I was pissed at Renee, I was pissed at the bank, I was pissed at myself for letting it happen. I remember going to the bank with copies of the checks and the manager of the bank basically laughing me out of his office telling me that I "didn't have a pot to piss in," that I could sue him or whatever I wanted, but I was out the money.

I got back to the office, told Martin what happened at the bank, and then I realized what I had to do about all of this. I had to go back to work. What was done was done. Worrying about revenge, getting pissed at the bank and all those "I'm going to get even and kick your ass thoughts" were basically just a waste of energy. No one was going to cover my obligations but me. I had to get my ass back to work, and do so quickly. That's exactly what I did.

As far as Renee Hardy? I haven't seen her since. I haven't talked to anyone who has seen or heard about her. I don't know if she is dead or alive. At this point she is just a footnote.

You never quite know in business if what you are doing is the right or wrong thing. Unfortunately, by the time you know the answer, someone has beaten you to it and you are out of business. I used to tell myself that it was okay to make little mistakes as long as I didn't make the big ones. I would continually search for new ideas. I read every book and magazine I could. Heck, three bucks for a magazine, twenty bucks for a book. One good idea would lead to a customer or a solution, and those magazines and books paid for themselves many times over. Some of the ideas I read were good, some not. In doing all the reading I learned a valuable lesson.

Everything I read was public. Anyone could buy the same books and magazines. The same information was available to anyone who wanted it. Turns out most people didn't want it.

I remember going into customer meetings or talking to people in the industry and tossing out tidbits about software or hardware. Features that worked, bugs in the software. All things I had read. I expected the ongoing

Teaching myself how to program. Notice the poster that says "Poverty Sucks" in the background!

response of: "Oh yeah, I read that too in such-and-such." That's not what happened. They hadn't read it then, and they still haven't started reading it.

Most people won't put in the time to get a knowledge advantage. Sure, there were folks that worked hard at picking up every bit of information that they could, but we were few and far between. To this day, I feel like if I put in enough time consuming all the information available, particularly with the Internet making it so readily accessible, I can get an advantage in any technology business. Of course, my wife hates that I read more than three hours almost every day, but it gives me a level of comfort and confidence in my businesses. At MicroSolutions it gave me a huge advantage. A guy with minimal computer background could compete with far more experienced guys just because he put in the time to learn all he could.

If I could come out of nowhere and be successful at the age of 24, so can you!

PART TWO:
LESSONS LEARNED

MY FIRST BUSINESS RULES

I learned from magazines and books, but I also learned from watching what some of the up-and-coming technology companies of the day were doing. It's funny how the companies that I thought were brilliant back then are still racking it up today.

Every week a company called PCs Limited used to take a full-page ad in a now internet only weekly trade magazine called *PC Week*. The ad would feature PC peripherals that the company would sell. Hard drives. Memory. Floppy drives. Graphics cards. Whatever could be added to a PC was there. What made the ad so special was that each and every week the prices got lower. If a drive was $2,000 dollars one week, it was $1,940 the next. For the first time in any industry that I knew of, we were seeing vendors pass on price savings to customers.

The PCs Limited ads became the "market price" for peripherals. I looked for the ad every week. In fact, I became a customer. I was in Dallas. They were in Austin.

I remember driving down to pick up some hard drives. I had no idea up to that point, but it turns out that they had just moved from the owner's dorm room into a little office/warehouse space. I was so impressed by this young kid (I was a wise, experienced 25-year-old at the time) that I actually wrote a letter thanking him for the great job he was doing, and ... I'm embarrassed to say now, I told him that if he kept up what he was doing he was destined for far bigger and better things.

I kept on doing business with PCs Limited, and Michael Dell. Yes, that Michael Dell, of Dell Computers. He kept on doing what he was doing. I don't think he really needed my encouragement, but I have since told him that I thought his weekly full page ads with ever-declining prices changed the PC industry and were the first of many genius moves on his part.

Michael Dell wasn't the only smart one in those days.

One of the PC industry's annual rituals was the Comdex trade show in Las Vegas. Every November, it was the only three days I knew I would get away and get a break from the office. It was work during the day. Visiting all the new technology booths. Trying to get better pricing from vendors. Trying to find out where the best parties were. If you could believe it, back in those days, the number one party was the Microsoft party. I sold some Microsoft products so I could get in.

One particular year, I was on my way to having a memorable night. I had met some very, very attractive women (I swear they were). Got them some tickets to come with me to the big party. All is good. I'm having fun. They're having fun. Then we see him. Bill G. As in Bill Gates. Dancing up a storm. I'm a Bill Gates fan, so I won't describe his dancing, but he was definitely having fun.

At that point in time, Microsoft had gone public and Bill Gates was Bill Gates. If you were in the business you knew him or knew of him. The girls I was with were in the business. Long story short, I go to the bar to get some drinks for all us and when I come back, they aren't there. Come to find out the next day, Bill stole my girls. As I would learn later in life, money makes you extremely handsome.

Bill G. also taught me a few things about business. Aside from how he killed IBM at its own game by licensing PC DOS to anyone who wanted it, what Microsoft did to knock Lotus 1-2-3 and WordPerfect off their thrones was literally business at its best.

At that point in time, software was expensive. WordPerfect and Lotus 1-2-3 both sold for $495.00 and their publishers were proud of that fact. In order to be able to sell Lotus 1-2-3 you had to go to special training to become authorized. How crazy does that sound? I literally was not allowed to sell a single copy of Lotus 1-2-3 until I passed their training class for the product.

WordPerfect, a word processing software wasn't quite as bad, but it had its own idiosyncrasies as well. Meanwhile, Microsoft was on the outside looking in. Excel, Word and

PowerPoint were all far down the list of top sellers until lightning struck.

Microsoft decided to go against industry protocol and package those three programs as a suite, offering them as an upgrade to competitors' products for the low, low price of $99. Of course, you needed to have and use Windows for it to work, but at a time when people were buying new PCs with every dramatic increase in power and decrease in price, it was a natural move for us at MicroSolutions to sell the bundle. It made the effective price of the PC and software together far, far lower. We loved it. It also taught me several big lessons.

LESSON #1:

Always ask yourself how someone could preempt your products or service. How can they put you out of business? Is it price? Is it service? Is it ease of use? No product is perfect and if there are good competitors in your market, they will figure out how to abuse you. It's always better if you are honest with yourself and anticipate where the problems will come from.

LESSON #2:

Always run your business like you are going to be competing with biggest technology companies in your industry—Google, Facebook, Oracle, Microsoft, whomever. They may not be your direct competitors. They may be a vendor. They may be a direct competitor *and* a vendor. Whatever they may be to your business, if you are in the technology business in any way shape or form, you have to anticipate that you will have to compete with one of them at some point. I ask myself every week what I would do if they entered any of my businesses. If you are ready to compete with the big guys, you are ready to compete with anyone else.

Watching the best taught me how to run my businesses. Along the way I taught myself a few things.

THE SPORT OF BUSINESS

I can't go more than a week without shooting baskets. There is something about the feel of the ball coming off my hand, the sound of the ball going through the net. It just feels good.

If I'm just standing in the gym, I can shoot pretty well. Playing in a game? Well, it's not quite what it used to be. I used to have a spin move that would work for me, no matter whom I was playing against or what level they were at. If I could get a pick and the defender went under, I didn't have to think about it, I could hit the shot. These days, my mind knows what to do, but my body just laughs at me. Put me up against 20-year-olds, and I won't embarrass myself, but it's only because I know how to set a pick and hit an open (a very wide-open) jumper, then spend the rest of the game getting out of the way.

I love to compete. I always have. Playing basketball was just something I had to do no matter how good I was, and it's something I will always do, no matter how old I get. It gives me a chance to blow off steam. It gives me a way to refocus.

But no matter how much I love to play the game or how involved and competitive I get during a Mavs game, it's only a minor release. Real competition comes from the sport of business.

In sports, you know who your opponents are. You know when you are going to play a game. You know pretty much how long the game will last. It's mentally and physically exhausting if you are at the top of the game, but it still pales in comparison to the effort required to be successful in business.

The sport of business isn't divided into games. It's not defined by practices. It doesn't have set rules that everyone plays by.

The sport of business is the ultimate competition.

It's 7 × 24 × 365 × forever.

I love the sport of business. I love the competition. I love the fire of it. It's the feeling of the clock winding down, the ball in your hands, and if you hit the shot you win … all day, every day.

Relaxing is for the other guy. I may be sitting in front of the TV, but I'm not watching it unless I think there is something I can learn from it. I'm thinking about things I can use in my business and the TV is just there.

I could take the time to read a fiction book, but I don't. I would rather read websites, newspapers, magazines, looking for ideas and concepts that I can use. I spend time in bookstores because one idea from a book or magazine can make me money.

I'm not going to go to dinner with you just to chat. I'm not going to give you a call to see how you are. Unless you want to talk business. Other guys play fantasy sports. I fire the synapses to get an edge.

That's what success is all about.
It's about the edge.

It's not whom you know. It's not how much money you have. It's very simple. It's whether or not you have the edge and have the guts to use it.

The edge is getting so jazzed about what you do, you just spent 24 hours straight working on a project and you thought only a couple of hours had passed.

The edge is knowing that you have to be the smartest guy in the room when you have your meeting and you are going to put in the effort to learn whatever you need to learn to get there.

The edge is knowing that when the four girlfriends you have had in the last couple years asked you which was more important, them or your business, you gave the right answer.

The edge is knowing that you can fail and learn from it, and just get back up and in the game.

The edge is knowing that people think you're crazy, and they are right, but you don't care what they think.

The edge is knowing how to blow off steam a couple times a week, just so you can refocus on business.

The edge is knowing that you are getting to your goals and treating people right along the way, because as good as you can be, you are so focused that you need regular people around you to balance and help you.

The edge is being able to confidently call out someone on a business issue because you have done your homework.

The edge is recognizing when you are wrong and working harder to make sure it doesn't happen again.

The edge is being able to drill down to identify issues and problems and solve them before anyone knows they are there.

The edge is knowing that while everyone else is

talking about nonsense like the "will to win" and how they know they *can* be successful, you are preparing yourself to compete so that you *will* be successful.

That's what makes business such an amazing sport. Everyone plays it. Everyone talks about how good he or she is or will be at it. Just a small percentage are.

Every single day someone has an idea. Every day someone talks about some business he wants to start. Every day someone is out there starting a business whose entire goal is to beat the hell out of yours. How cool is that?!

Every day some stranger somewhere in the world is trying to come up with a way to put you out of business. To take everything you have worked your ass off for, just take it all away. If you are in a growing industry, there could be hundreds or thousands of strangers trying to figure out ways to put you out of business. How cool is that?!

The ultimate competition. Would you like to play a game called Eat Your Lunch? We are going to face off. My ability to execute an idea vs. yours. My ability to subvert your business vs. your ability to keep it going. My ability to create ways to remove any reason for your business to exist vs. your ability to do the same to me. My ability to know what you are going to do, before you do it vs. you, er, doing it! Who gets there first? Best of all, this game doesn't have a time limit. It's forever. It never ends. It's the ultimate competition.

It's the sport of business. It's not for everyone, but I love it.

I'm fortunate. I have done well enough financially that I don't have to play 24 × 7 × 365. I can and have cut back to 18 × 7 × 365. Family first, now.

But in those eighteen hours, you can bet I'm competing and loving it.

But that's me. You have to figure out what works for you.

THE ONE THING IN LIFE YOU CAN CONTROL: EFFORT

I remember the time well. I was 27 years old.

I finally had my own apartment for the first time. I still hadn't bought a new car yet, but I was jazzed that I had a four-year-old Mazda RX-7. Four years old was as good as new to me, and driving a gold RX-7 back in the day was fun as well.

I had upgraded my wardrobe from my 2 for $99 dollar polyester suits to a couple really cool, brand name suits. Of course I bought them used. I could care less that someone had worn them before. One trip to the drycleaners and as far as I was concerned, they were brand new. Although by then I did have one new suit made of natural materials that I had bought at Neiman Marcus because my girlfriend worked there and brought me to one of their year-end employee discount deals.

My business, MicroSolutions, was a little more than three years old, and I would make $60K that year. HUGE money for me. Back then, getting paid your age was good, double your age was great.

Around Christmas of that year, after many welcomed hints from my then-girlfriend, I decided to take every penny I had in my savings, $7,500; buy a ring —a beautiful ring; and get engaged.

Long story short? I gave her the ring. A couple weeks later while we were still blissfully happy, we went to a movie. I'm sure it was a great movie. Unfortunately the next day she realized she had lost the ring. Of course she was incredibly upset to lose the ring. I was upset because I had not insured it yet. Maybe it was an omen. Long story short, a little while later we broke up. (The upshot is that I was too young to get married and we are still good friends).

So there I was, 27 years old. The ring on which I had spent every penny I had probably sat in a pawnshop somewhere in Dallas. I was left with zero in the bank. The good news was that I had my business. The one thing that I could always focus on to the exclusion of everything else. A trait that would serve me well in business, but had more than a little bit to do with my breakup.

MicroSolutions was growing, but it could have been doing better. The PC industry had gone through a major slump and pullback, and the local area networking industry had yet to take off. If we were going to grow, it was going to take working hard and working smart.

It was right around then I heard something that I would hear a lot once I bought the Mavs.

In sports, the only thing a player can truly control is

effort. The same applies to business. The only thing any entrepreneur, salesperson or anyone in any position can control is their effort.

I had to kick myself in the ass and recommit to getting up early, staying up late and consuming everything I possibly could to get an edge. I had to commit to making the effort to be as productive as I possibly could.

> **It meant making sure that every hour of the day that I could contact a customer was selling time, and when customers were sleeping, I was doing things that prepared me to make more sales and to make my company better.**

And finally, I had to make sure I wasn't lying to myself about how hard I was working. It would have been easy to judge effort by how many hours a day passed while I was at work. That's the worst way to measure effort. Effort is measured by setting goals and getting results. What did I need to do to close this account? What did I need to do to win this segment of business? What did I need to do to understand this technology or that business better than

Of course a great effort meant looking the part when I was giving a presentation at MicroSolutions!

anyone? What did I need to do to find an edge? Where does that edge come from, and how was I going to get there?

The one requirement for success in our business lives is effort. Either you make the commitment to get results or you don't.

SCATTERBRAINED AND IN COLLEGE

BEING FOCUSED AT 21 IS OVERRATED

Here's to all the college kids out there who are pretty much the same as I was.

> *Dear Mark,*
>
> *I was in the group that listened to you speak at the X. And I need some guidance, dude. I don't know if you've ever experienced addictive behavior before, but I'm sure you've got an idea of what it would be like. Now I want to specify that I'm not addicted to drugs or alcohol or any of that junk. I'm addicted to adventure. To pushing physical boundaries and experiencing new things. But man, it's killing me right*

now. I can't focus on anything that I need to do. I'm a full-time undergrad and a real estate agent (among other things), and this desperate search for adventure is not driving me toward my goals; it is crippling me.

Before you had the freedom to do whatever you want, whenever you want, how did you maintain focus on the things you needed to do?

My response:

You are still in school. You don't need to have all the answers or focus on one thing. You should be trying a lot of things until you find the one thing you really love to do and are good at. When that happens, you will be able to focus.

Being focused at 21 is way overrated. Now is the time to screw up, to try as many different things as you can and just maybe figure things out.

The thing you do need to do is learn. Learn accounting. Learn finance. Learn statistics. Learn as much as you can about business. Read biographies about businesspeople. You don't have to focus on one thing, but you have to create a base of knowledge so you are ready when it's time.

You never know when that time will come. But you can be ready when it does. You never know, you might end up in the adventure business!

WHAT ARE YOU DESTINED TO BE?

Every day I get at least one email from someone proclaiming that they are "destined to be" X. You can fill in the blank with any number of dreams the person has for himself: to be rich, famous, the best this or that. Of course they aren't emailing me just to tell me; they are emailing to ask for money to enable them to be whatever it is they dream of being. But it leads to questions. Do we know what we are destined to be or do we find out through experience? Are each of us really good at something, and it's just a matter of discovering it? Do we all have something that we would love to do every day, and do we inherently know it or do we have to find it? Will what you love to do be the same as what you are great at?

Personally, I always have enjoyed business, but I never knew that I had an aptitude for technology until I got a job at Mellon Bank that lasted all of eight months. But during the many hours of boredom, I found myself sitting in front of a mainframe teaching myself a scripting language called RAMIS and loving every minute of it. Which led to me buying a TI-99A, I think it was, for $79, attaching a tape recorder as a drive (how is that for dating myself) and teaching myself BASIC. Which led to ... well, you get the idea. I loved every minute of it. Maybe I wasn't the best programmer in the world, but in combination with business and sales skills, I found something that was a blast to me that I could and did do 24 hours at a time and not miss a beat.

If you're asking, I don't think people "know" what they are destined to be until they try it for the first couple of times.

> **Going to college should be about experiencing as much academically as you possibly can, but more importantly, it should be about learning how to learn and recognizing that learning is a lifelong endeavor. School isn't the end of the learning process, it's purely a training ground and beginning.**

In my humble opinion, once you have learned how to learn, then you can try as many different things as you can, recognizing that you don't have to find your destiny at any given age—you just have to be prepared to run with it when you do.

Of course, there is always a caveat to destiny, and that's

obligation. The greatest obstacle to destiny is debt, both personal and financial. The more people you are obligated to, the harder it is to focus on yourself and figure things out. I'm a big believer that getting married is about finding yourself first, which makes it a lot easier to find the right person. If you can't stand on your own, it's impossible to successfully be part of a couple.

I'm also a big believer that financial debt is the ultimate dream killer. Your first house, car, whatever you might want to buy, is going to be the primary reason you stop looking for what makes you the happiest.

How crazy is it to settle for a house, car or X over what it is you would like to do on an hourly or daily basis?

Never settle. There is no reason to rush.

If you aren't happy with where you are, simplify your life and go out and try as many things as it takes to find what you may be destined to be. If there is such a thing.

YOU ONLY HAVE TO BE RIGHT ONCE!

In basketball you have to shoot 50 percent. If you make an extra 10 shots per hundred, you are an All-Star. In baseball you have to get a hit 30 percent of the time. If you get an extra 10 hits per hundred at bats, you are on the cover of every magazine, lead off every SportsCenter and make the Hall of Fame.

In business, the odds are a little different. You don't have to break the Mendoza Line (hitting .200). In fact, it doesn't matter how many times you strike out. In business, to be a success, you only have to be right once.

One single time and you are set for life. That's the beauty of the business world.

I like to tell the story of how I started my first business at age 12, selling garbage bags. No one ever has asked if I was any good or made money at it. Yes, I was, and yes, I did … enough to buy some tennis shoes, anyway.

The line to get into Motley's Pub—my senior project.

We had a lot of fun at Motley's…

Until we got busted for underage drinking because this girl turned out to be on probation for prostitution at the ripe old age of 16.

I like to tell the story of how I started a bar, Motley's Pub, when I wasn't even of legal drinking age the summer before my senior year at Indiana University. No one really asks me how it turned out. It was great until we got busted for letting a 16-year-old win a wet T-shirt contest. (I swear I checked her ID, and it was good!)

No one really asks me about my adventures working for Mellon Bank, or Tronics 2000, or trying to start a business selling powdered milk (it was cheaper by the gallon, and I thought it tasted good enough). They don't ask me about working nights as a bartender at Elan's when I first got to Dallas, or getting fired from my job at Your Business Software for wanting to close a sale rather than open up the store.

No one ever asks me about what it was like when I started MicroSolutions or how I used to count the months I was in business, hoping to outlast my previous endeavors and make this one a success.

With every effort, I learned a lot. With every mistake and failure (not only mine, but also of those around me), I learned what not to do. I also got to study the success of those with whom I did business. I had more than a healthy dose of fear, an unlimited amount of hope and, more importantly, no limit on time or effort.

Fortunately, things turned out well for me with MicroSolutions. I sold it after seven years and made enough money to take time off and have a whole lot of fun.

I vividly remember people telling me how lucky I was to sell MicroSolutions at the right time.

Then, when I took that money and started trading technology stocks that were in the areas that MicroSolutions

Celebrating the sale
of MicroSolutions to
CompuServe with
Martin Woodall

focused on, I vividly remember being told how lucky I was to have expertise in such a hot area, as technology stocks started to trade up.

Of course, no one wanted to comment on how lucky I was to spend countless hours reading software or Cisco Router manuals, or sitting in my house testing and comparing new technologies, but that's a topic for another time.

The point of all this is that it doesn't matter how many times you fail. It doesn't matter how many times you almost get it right. No one is going to know or care about your failures, and neither should you. All you have to do is learn from them and from those around you because ...

All that matters in business is that you get it right once.

Then everyone can tell you how lucky you are.

WHAT I LEARNED FROM BOBBY KNIGHT

There are a lot of things I could say thank you for. The great times watching IU basketball (even though I wasn't a fan when I got there—I thought any team with Kent Benson *should* go undefeated). Learning that focus and intensity can be virtues and conduits to success.

When I first met you at IU at the Dean's residence, where they tried to butter me up for a donation and you were mad that they made you dress up while I showed up wearing jeans.

The time you spent talking to me down in Miami.

But that's not really what I appreciate most about you.

When I was at Indiana you appeared on *60 Minutes*. In your interview you said one thing that I truly took to heart. I reminded myself of it while it was in school. I reminded myself of it before starting any of the many businesses I have begun. I remind myself of it whenever I fail. I will continue to remind myself of it before any of my endeavors going forward. It's the best advice I've been able to give people of any age who ask me for advice.

It's also the characteristic I look for when choosing a partner or when hiring an employee or coach. I saw it in Avery Johnson. I saw it in Rick Carlisle. I've seen it in Phil Garvin. It was obvious in Todd Wagner and Martin Woodall and many, many others who have put me in a position to succeed.

You said, and I'm paraphrasing:

"Everyone has got the will to win; it's only those with the will to *prepare* that do win."

Words for every athlete and those of us who partake in the Sport of Business to live by.

Thanks, Coach.

DROWNING IN OPPORTUNITY / WINNING THE BATTLES YOU ARE IN

There are few things more exciting than starting a business and getting things rolling. The fear, the adrenaline, the excitement, the hope that every entrepreneur feels ... all are intoxicating. In fact, very often they are TOO intoxicating. Very often, along with some success comes the feeling of invincibility. I have been in situations where I have told myself that I'm smart, I know what I'm doing, that I will figure things out as I go, so it's okay to take on this new opportunity. Those were usually the times I made mistakes.

In a lifetime of running businesses I have developed a lot of rules that have been almost infallible. Here are a few of them that I use religiously to this day:

I. EVERYONE IS A GENIUS IN A BULL MARKET

A lot of people think that if they are picking stocks that keep on going up, it's because they are smart. They fail to notice that EVERYONE is able to pick winning stocks when all stocks are going up. The same principle applies to business. Entrepreneurs have to be brutally honest with themselves and recognize where they have added value and where they have gone along for the ride. There is nothing wrong with going along for the ride and making money at it, but it will catch up with you if you lie to yourself and give yourself credit for the ride.

Sports leagues are the perfect examples from an industry that thought it was responsible for growth, when in reality it was a bull market for rights fees.

First, the advent of cable created competition for sports rights, which in turn increased the value of sports rights. Then satellite television came along, which created increased competition for cable and broadcast for sports rights, so values went up again. Then the competition between rights holders who created their own regional sports networks once more increased the value of sports rights. Today, sports are in a sweet spot because of the rise in adoption of TiVo and similar technologies by TV viewers. Sports is the most TiVo-resistant programming.

Smart sports rights holders, such as we are trying to be with the Mavericks, recognize that it wasn't our brilliance that to this point had pushed up our television rights revenues. It was the market. It's our challenge to recognize what we can do to push the value of our programming further. It's a bigger challenge to recognize that the bull market may end and our programming needs to be of sufficient value to our customers and viewers for it to maintain or continue to increase in value.

It's also our challenge to recognize when there is opportunity. Sports is one of the few TiVo-proof programming options for advertisers. We have a unique chance to lever up our viewership to prove our value as a TiVo-proof option to advertisers by integrating value for our advertisers into our games and by working to increase our viewership. It's critical not just because we want to protect and increase this revenue stream, but because across our revenue streams it has the most upside. Advertisers want a way to stay in front of the largest possible TiVo-proof audiences, with the unique experience of HDTV, congregating at the same time, rather than picking them off one at a time in an on-demand universe. One gives you a number the next morning, the other takes a long time to aggregate into an audience size of value. That makes it a unique opportunity the Mavs have to work hard to leverage with our partners.

For the Mavs, it's also important to realize that we can't raise ticket prices forever without pricing ourselves out of the market. In fact, we lowered the price of all tickets in our upper bowl and created a $2 ticket (I repeat, that's TWO DOLLARS) for 10 of our games. Fans can get 10 games for $20. That lowering of ticket prices is the most powerful, least expensive marketing we can do. It leads to a more positive brand value and greater commitment to the Mavs, which helps us create new products that leverage the live nature of our product.

It's not easy, but we recognize that our past increases in revenues were frequently as much the result of industry trends as of our efforts. We have to make sure to do whatever we can to focus on winning the battles in case the bull market does not continue.

Which leads to Rule #2 ...

2. WIN THE BATTLES YOU ARE IN BEFORE YOU TAKE ON NEW BATTLES

Every one of my businesses has a make-or-break battle going on, and so does yours. There is one battle in your business that you are not winning, or are battling to stay in front.

In our film business, it's the battle to bring in more box office than we spend getting people to theaters in the first place. With the Mavs, it's the battle to make our game experience in the arena and on TV so compelling that it's strong enough entertainment on its own to draw an audience and make our advertisers happy. I can't control how a game on the court goes, but I can make sure that if you come to a game or watch one on the tube, you have a great time. At HDNet, it's how to keep on raising the bar and find or create programming that our subscribers feel committed to and take ownership of. I can spend as much money on a show as a big network, but those big networks are wrong 95 percent of the time. It's not a model I want to copy. It's the ultimate challenge to find a new way to get results.

These literally are the three problems that I focus on. They aren't issues that just popped up. They have been challenges in these businesses for years and present moving targets that require my ongoing focus, today and most likely for years to come. It's an intellectual challenge I really love. It's truly the sport of business. Sure, I deal with operational issues, but pretty much every other strategic element of my businesses **I have learned to delegate**—that's not easy for an entrepreneur to do. In the past, I would have taken on anything and everything that I thought I could add value to. I had to be in the middle of everything. No longer. **I've learned to hire people in whom I can build trust, and let them take the ball and run with it.**

Of course, not every business has bench strength. Some entrepreneurs won't hire people who have complementary skill sets. Others are just small businesses that can't afford it yet. For those businesses, this rule is all the more important. If you are the main engine behind your company, taking on new challenges will only dilute your ability to win the wars you are in and increase the risk of injuring your primary business or core competencies.

In fact, this is the biggest issue I have with the NBA and our international efforts. It's not that I think there is no opportunity internationally—there is. The problem is that the "CEO" of the NBA is at the front and in the middle of every effort. His efforts are diluted on both domestic and international fronts, and we risk losing multiple important battles. If the metrics for the lines of our business that drive 75 percent or more of our business were skyrocketing, that would be one thing. But we aren't winning the battles we are in. We aren't losing, we aren't winning, we're just treading water.

International isn't going anywhere. China, for example, has great potential and it always will. If we were dominating in our core revenue lines, I could easily be the biggest proponent of an international NBA effort (short of contributing our players to competitive enterprises). The NBA needs to find someone who can lead and win each of the battles. Trying to use one person as the leader for both is a huge mistake that is not worth the risk it exposes us to.

I have used the same logic with HDNet. HDTV is taking hold all over the world. In many areas it's booming. We sell content to those flourishing markets via salespeople, but I have said "no" to offers to bring HDNet to the rest of the world as a linear or online network. Why? Because dealing with the rest of the world takes a lot of time and focus. It takes going out and hiring people to run it, and training them and then being available to help support their efforts on an ongoing basis. Every minute that I or our top people spend dealing with the rest of the world is a minute not spent fighting the battle to make HDNet and HDNet Movies the best networks they can be here in the U.S. We are not a business that has maximized our growth here; we are just starting to accelerate.

Taking any resources away from that battle would be a huge mistake.

It's the same with Landmark Theaters. We could go international, but winning the battles here is far more important and, again, every minute our leadership spends on the rest of the world is time and focus lost on Landmark in the U.S.

It's a huge lesson for entrepreneurs. **Win the battles you are in first, then worry about expansion internationally or into new businesses.** You do not have unlimited time and/or attention. You may work 24 hours a day, but those 24 hours spent winning your core business will pay off far more. It might cost you some longer-term upside, but it will allow you to be the best business you can be. To use a sports metaphor, get the fundamentals right and then add to your base skills before you try to take on the trick shots.

Rule #3 is the natural extension of Rule #2.

3. YOU CAN DROWN IN OPPORTUNITY

Few businesses only have one opportunity. Every entrepreneur's mind goes crazy with the new and exciting things she can do beyond the new and exciting things she is already doing. The risk is that you can drown in all these opportunities. Far too often when an entrepreneur hits a rough patch or competitive challenge, the temptation is to "turn on the thinking cap" and find something new for the company to do. Don't fall prey to the temptation. As an entrepreneur you have to know what the core competencies of your business are and make sure that your company focuses on being the absolute best it can be at executing them. Bottom line is this: If you are adding new things when your core businesses are struggling rather than facing the challenge, you are either running away or giving up. Rarely is either good for a business. In fact, by chasing these opportunities, you may be assuring that you drown in them.

These rules are things I check off against before I undertake new elements of a business.

DON'T LIE TO YOURSELF

I learned a lot from Don Nelson when he was coach and GM of the Mavericks. He told me something early on that opened my eyes. I forget the exact conversation, but we were talking about players, and I asked him why he didn't talk to a specific player about something that was going on. What he said was, "The worst evaluator of talent is a player trying to evaluate himself."

The same applies to businesspeople and particularly to entrepreneurs and wannabe entrepreneurs. We tend to be less than honest with ourselves about our strengths and weaknesses.

I have been just as bad at this as anyone, particularly when I was getting started in the business world. For those of us who dream of starting and running a business, we know that we have to have a level of confidence in our own abilities. We don't want to believe that there are things we can't do. We want to believe that if we try hard enough, work long enough and get a little lucky, that the sky is the limit. The problem is that we let our confidence cloud our judgment of what we truly know about ourselves.

I'm one of the least organized people I know. Today, I have an assistant and others that help me run my life. If you ask me where I'm going to be in three days, I have no idea. I do know that I have a kick-ass assistant who is going to make sure that when I wake up that morning, I know where I'm going and how to get there.

When I was 23 years old, sleeping on the floor and starting MicroSolutions, there was no assistant. Thus, there was no organization. I was a procrastinator. Accounting was a shoebox of receipts. I was a mess.

But I lied to myself and said that I could deal with it. That I would make time to get it all figured out and organized. That if I only set my mind to it, I could be a details person. I could stop procrastinating. It doesn't work that way.

I did the things I was good at. I could sell. So I sold. I could write software programs. I could integrate PCs. I could set up local area networks. And I did. My business grew. But it also grew out of control. A local area network or a software program without documentation is a disaster waiting to happen. And disasters did happen. Not to the point where it killed my business, but to the point where I spent far too much time fixing things rather than selling new deals.

Fortunately, one of my best customers at the time was interested in becoming a partner in my business. Martin Woodall ran a company called Hytec Data Systems. He was not only smart and a good programmer, but he was the most anal, detail-oriented person I had ever met in my life. The perfect partner for me.

Our partnership wasn't always easy. We had more than our share of knock-down, drag-out fights. He, of course, would want everything done with precision, and if lack of perfection was an option, he didn't want to do it. I, of course, was the exact opposite. I was the GO FOR IT guy. The "we can sort it out after the fact" guy. We were perfect partners. We knew and trusted the skills of the other, and although many might not think yelling was the best way to work things out, we managed.

It all came down to choice. I had the choice between lying to myself and pretending that I could turn on a switch and become a details person, or accepting the fact that I'm not, and partnering with someone who is. Continuing to lie meant I would probably lose my business.

Every entrepreneur faces comparable choices. Each of us has to face the reality of who we are and what we are.

What choice will you make?

THE BEST EQUITY IS SWEAT EQUITY

As MicroSolutions became more and more successful, and as I paid attention to the common traits of businesses I saw succeed and those I saw fail, I came to realize that there were "Rules of Success" in the companies that excelled. When companies failed to follow those rules, they inevitably failed. I found myself checking with The Rules before I made decisions. When I traded stocks or considered investments in companies, I applied The Rules to these businesses before I made a decision.

The Rules are not infallible. They have their limits. I'm an entrepreneur. My businesses have had hundreds and now more than a thousand employees. My world has been limited to starting, building, growing and running businesses that are never going to make the Fortune 500. My dreams were never to build the biggest corporation in the world. So, if you are a middle level manager in a Fortune 500 company, these rules may not help you manage your department. If you are the CEO of a Fortune 500 company with tens of thousands of employees, some rules will apply and some won't, but where they will help you is to know how little guys coming out of nowhere are going to disrupt your business.

Where The Rules will really come into play is if you are considering starting, or currently run, your own business. There are always exceptions to any rules, but I can assure you that in this case, those exceptions will be rare. Entrepreneurs who don't follow The Rules are far more likely to fail. There is no doubt about it.

So let's start at the beginning. In this post I am only going to provide you with the very first and most important of all the rules for anyone starting a business.

Rule #1: Sweat equity is the best startup capital

The best businesses in recent entrepreneurial history are those that began with little or no money. Dell Computers, Microsoft, Compaq, Apple, HP and tens of thousands of others started in dorm rooms, tiny offices or garages. There weren't 100-page-long business plans. In all of my businesses, I started by putting together spreadsheets of my expenses, which allowed me to calculate how much revenue I needed to break even and keep the lights on in my office and my apartment. I wrote overviews of what I was selling, why I thought the business made sense, an overview of my competition, why my product and/or service would be important to my customers and why they should buy or use it. All of it went down on a piece of yellow paper or in a word processing file, and none of it cost me more than the diet soda I was drinking while I was writing it up.

I remember the foundation for each of my businesses. MicroSolutions was very simple—to use microcomputers and software to help our customers become more productive and profitable and gain a competitive advantage. AudioNet, which became Broadcast.com, was simple as well: Use the Internet to enable real-time, worldwide communications of entertainment and business applications. HDNet's goal is to create great entertainment, originated in high-definition format, that allows our distributors to compete for the highest-margin customers.

Once I could put the idea on paper, I gave the company a name. From there, I took the most important step: I tried to find people to shoot holes in the name. When we started AudioNet, I remember getting an appointment with Drew Marcus of Alex. Brown (it could have been Larry, but I think it was Drew), an investment banking company. Drew followed the radio industry, and I wanted to see if there was anything he saw from his experience that would blow up the concept.

He loved the idea. We took it to Dan Halliburton of Susquehanna Radio. He was an executive in charge of several Dallas-area radio stations. We discussed how he could broadcast his stations over the Internet using AudioNet and reach the in-office market where there weren't many radios on desks, and the few that existed would rarely pick up the AM signal of his stations. He loved it. I took it to Tim and Eric Crown, who ran a newly public company called Insight Enterprises. I asked them if it made sense to broadcast their quarterly-earning conference calls over the Internet so their investors and the research analysts who followed them could easily listen to the calls and get up-to-date information, or listen to an archive of the call if they missed it. They thought it would help them reach their Investor Relation goals less expensively.

Each inquiry cost me next to nothing to get great feedback. Each enabled me to check the foundation of my business idea to see if it was easy to shoot holes in, and most importantly, they all served as sales calls. Each company eventually became a customer of ours.

I went through this in each of my businesses. The step gave me confidence that my business idea was valid. That there was a chance of success. At this point, many entrepreneurs think the next step is to take all this feedback, update their 100-page business plans and go out and raise money. It's as if the missing link for success in a business is cash to get started. It's not. Far more often than not, raising cash is the biggest mistake you can make.

Most entrepreneurs tend to think in terms of what raising money means to them. How it can get them started. How many people they can hire. How much they can spend on office space. How much they can pay themselves. They forget to put themselves in the position of the person or company they are asking for money. They think they are considering that person's position by making up numbers and calling them expected returns for the investor. "If you only give me X dollars, you will get Y percent back in Z years. You will double or triple your money in XX years." Any investor worth anything knows you are just making these numbers up. They are meaningless. Worse, if you tell a savvy investor that the market for your product is X billions of dollars and you just need one or some low percent to make zillions, you will be immediately kicked to the curb.

These investors, including myself, know what you don't, and they are not telling you. The minute you ask for money, you are playing in their game—they aren't playing in yours. You are at a huge disadvantage, and it's only going to get worse if you take their money. The minute you take money, the leverage completely flips to the investor. They control the destiny of your dreams, not you.

Investors don't care about your dreams and goals. They love that you have them. They love that you are motivated by them. Investors care about how they are going to get their money back and then some. Family cares about your dreams. Investors care about money. There is a reason why venture capitalists are often referred to as Vulture Capitalists. The minute you slide off course from the promises you made to get the money, your dreams fall in jeopardy. You will find yourself making promises to keep investors at bay. You will find yourself avoiding your investors. Then you will find yourself on the outside looking in. The reality of taking money from non-family members is that they are doing it for only one reason, to make more money. If you can't deliver on that promise, you are out. You will be removed from the company you started. You will find someone else running your dream company. If this sounds like a scene out of *The Sopranos* or some TV episode about a loan shark, you are right. The only difference is that it's all legal.

There are only two reasonable sources of capital for

With Todd Wagner in the early days of AudioNet, which became Broadcast.com

Rehearsing for *Dancing with the Stars*

startup entrepreneurs: your own pocket and your customers' pockets. I personally would never even take money from a family member. Could you imagine the eternal grief and guilt from your mom, dad, uncle or aunt because you blew your nephew's college fund or the money for grandma's last vacation? I can't.

You shouldn't have to take money from anyone. Businesses don't have to start big. The best ones start small enough to suit the circumstances of their founders. I started

MicroSolutions by getting an advance of $500 from my first customer. The business didn't grow quickly in the first couple years—just up to four people, and we all worked dirt cheap.

So what's wrong with that? Nothing! **It's okay to start slow. It's okay to grow slow.** As much as you want to think that all things would change if you only had more cash available, they probably won't.

The reality is that for most businesses, they don't need more cash, they need more brains.

WHAT WILL YOU REMEMBER WHEN YOU ARE 90?

Unique opportunities. How many of them will you have in your life? One? One hundred? The thing about life is that it's impossible to know. You never know when something you never even considered *could* happen, *will* happen.

As someone who has been incredibly blessed, let me just tell you that the things at the top of my list are not numbers or dollars. They are my family and the things I had fun doing.

A lot of people think I'm crazy, or chasing publicity, or whatever. I don't care what they think.

Before I do any of the many things that I get asked to do, and that I think might be fun, I have one simple question I ask myself. When I (hopefully) turn 90 and look back at my life, would I regret having done it, or not having done it?

Before I started Motley's Pub with Evan Williams when we were at Indiana University and I wasn't even old enough to drink, this was the question I asked myself. Before we sold MicroSolutions. Before I spent the money to buy a lifetime pass on American Airlines when I was 29 and then retired to travel the world. Before I bought the Mavs. Before I did *The Benefactor* on ABC, or *Dancing with the Stars*, or *Survivor*, or WWE's *Raw*, or any number of other fun and amazing things. It's the question I have always asked myself. To me it's part of being successful.

When I'm 90, will I smile when I think back, or will I frown and regret not having done it? Success is about making your life a special version of unique that fits who you are—*not* what other people want you to be.

CONNECTING TO YOUR CUSTOMERS

I have a couple of customer service sayings I tend to over-use. I don't usually speak them out loud. I usually say them to myself as a reminder to always put our customers, in any business, first.

"Treat your customers like they own you. Because they do." "You have to re-earn your customers business every day." And there's one that came from Yahoo!, which I thought was brilliant. When asked what Yahoo! stood for, some folks there responded, "You Always Have Other Options."

I personally think that the only way you can connect to your customers is to put yourself in their shoes. For me personally, if I can't be a customer of my own product, then I probably am not going to do a good job running the company. When I go to a Landmark Theater, I don't call ahead and tell them I'm coming so I can get special treatment. I stand in line and pay for my ticket like everyone else. I get my popcorn and Diet Coke like everyone else. I get my seat like everyone else.

With the Mavs, I sit in a seat that is for sale to the general public. Yes, it's a great seat next to the bench, but I also make sure that I sit in the very top row behind the baskets, in our $2-10 seats, during the season. Same routine. I'm not surrounded by security. I don't get special anything. If the nachos are slow to come and the beer is warm, I know it, and the people sitting around me also let me know.

It's interesting to watch different CEOs of different companies and how they deal with the issue of making customers happy. You can tell the ones that don't trust their products or services. They travel with big groups of people. There are advance teams to make sure everything is perfect. They bring security to places where their customers are families and kids. They protect themselves from any possible interaction, whether direct, phone or email, by having secretaries filter everything, and they respond with form letters or through assistants, if at all.

I don't know how they do it. I make my email available to everyone and anyone. Not only that (and more importantly), I make sure that all the customer service emails get forwarded to me. If someone is complaining, I want to know about it, and I want to get it fixed quickly. The best focus groups are your customers telling you what they think. No company is perfect, but the CEO who doesn't listen to direct feedback from customers will not take the company as far as it can go.

But it gets worse from there for CEOs who don't communicate with their customers. There used to be a saying that happy customers might tell one person, but unhappy customers tell 20. In the Internet age, one happy customer might make a note in their blog or forward an email. An unhappy customer starts a blog, writes about how unhappy he is, takes out an ad on search engines to let people who are looking for the product know how mad he is, starts an email forwarding chain asking people to boycott the product, does a YouTube video about it and games YouTube to make it one of the Top 10 most-viewed videos ... You get the picture.

In this day and age, it's a lot easier to proactively communicate than to react.

IT'S OK TO BE A WHINER

I'm a whiner. I guess I finally have to admit it. I took a look back at the way I have lived my life, and I can't come to any other conclusion.

When I was in high school, I whined about not being able to take business classes my junior year (they were only available to seniors), so I took classes at the University of Pittsburgh instead.

When I got to Indiana University, I whined that the classes they wanted me to take weren't enough of a challenge, so I snuck into the MBA program and took graduate-level statistics when I was a freshman. Then I took other MBA-level classes as a freshman and sophomore, which gave me the confidence to compete at any level.

When I got a job selling software, I whined to the owner that he shouldn't make me sweep the floor of our store and I should be able to go out and close sales. That led to me getting fired, which in turn led to me starting MicroSolutions.

When I started MicroSolutions, I whined that there were no companies that could help hook personal computers together, so we became one of the first integrators for Novell Share Data Systems, which in turn became the core for our business that grew and grew until I sold it in 1990 and retired for a few years.

When I was hanging out with my buddy Todd Wagner, we whined together about how we couldn't listen to Indiana Basketball or any hometown sports in Dallas, so we started AudioNet, which became Broadcast.com.

When I was at opening night of the Mavs 1999-2000 season, I whined to my friends that there was no energy, no fun in the building, that I could do a better job. Which led to me buying the Mavs.

When I bought my first HDTV, I whined about the fact that there was no content, which led to me starting HDNet with Phil Garvin.

Now that I own the Mavs, I whine about a lot of things in the NBA, from marketing to officials, which has led to change. Changes in how games are sold and marketed, how games are presented, how some departments are organized and managed in the NBA. That's the nice thing about whining to an organization that wants to improve. They might not always show the love, but actions can speak louder than words.

When we started producing movies, I whined that it made no sense that movies couldn't be released in theaters, on HDNet and on DVD and HD DVD all on the same day. So we started releasing movies day and date (in other words, simultaneously).

I'm sure there have been many other things I have whined about in the past, and many more that I will whine about in the future. **What I don't understand is why so many people think whining has a negative connotation. I don't.**

Whining is the first step toward change. It's the moment when you realize something is very wrong and that you have to take the initiative to do something about it. Sure, criticism usually comes along with the territory. Who cares?

People in media like to call people whiners. With a negative connotation. Because, of course, people in the media are nonwhiners. Which they, amazingly enough, think is a good thing.

People who don't whine are punching bags. They just go about their days, their jobs, their lives, knowing there is nothing they can do to change a darn thing, so why say a word? They see no reason to whine because they know they are incapable of effecting change.

Call me a whiner any day.

THE PATH OF
LEAST RESISTANCE

I recently read an article by Paul Kagan referring to George Gilder's "vision" that in the future TV will die, regardless of delivery medium, simply because people will watch only what they want to watch.

How wrong he is. Why he is wrong is a lesson in basic business.

It was Aaron Spelling, I believe, who said, "TV is the path of least resistance from complete boredom." Which is another way of saying that it's easier to watch TV than to sit there and do nothing. Which describes exactly how people make most of their choices in life. They take the easy way. They take the path of least resistance. There are certain things in life we all have to do. There are certain things in life we choose to do. Then there is everything else. The things we do to kill time.

In every case, all things being equal, we choose the path of least resistance.

Understanding this concept is key to making good business decisions.

When Broadcast.com was around, we understood that our strength came from being the path of least resistance for out-of-market sports that weren't available on national TV. If we had the option of offering a football game that was going to be on national TV in the evening, it wouldn't matter how good the game was. No one was going to choose to listen online because it was easier to watch on TV.

If that same game was on during a weekday afternoon when most people were at work, we knew that we would get a great audience because it was easier for people stuck in their offices to listen on their PCs than to try to sneak out of the office and get to a TV. Offering content for which the path of least resistance was watching or listening online was a key to our building an audience.

The path of least resistance is key to why HDNet Films offers our slate of films in a variety of day-and-date options.

For the couple who wants to go on a date, going to a theater is often the path of least resistance for an easy, relatively inexpensive evening together.

For the family who wants to see the movie but can't make it out of the house for whatever reason, getting it on HDNet Movies or through day-and-date delivery of a DVD is the path of least resistance. We feel that people will pay a premium to be able to stay at home and watch those movies, either by subscribing to HDNet or by paying more than the traditional retail price of a DVD. It's easier to pay a premium for access to the movie than to deal with the kids screaming about not being able to go. So we gear the movies we make to an adult audience. Enough people can get out of the house to see the movie, preferably in a Landmark Theater. Enough have kids, can't get out and have disposable income, so they are more likely to order the DVD or subscribe to HDNet Movies in order to see what they want to see. We want to offer our movies in the path of least resistance for our target demographic.

The path of least resistance is why I think Amazon. com, Apple and Google have been so successful.

I buy everything from books to electronics to toiletries on Amazon because it's easier than schlepping to the store. They show up in the mail as quickly as I am willing to pay to have them show up.

I got my iPod and gave iTunes my credit card. It now takes me seconds to sample and download music. To the extreme that I even downloaded songs from the Wiggles so that my daughter could listen to them while I was working. It was the path of least resistance to keeping her occupied so I could get my work done.

Google one-upped Yahoo! a few years ago by making it simple and easy to plug in a search and get results. Yahoo! made us scan through their home page to make a search and often took us to directories and other intermediaries. Google was the path of least resistance for simple searches.

TiVo has been successful because it has made it so easy to record the shows we want to see. The show comes on, you hit a button. You decide if it's just this show, or if you want to subscribe for the season. The path of least resistance for time-shifting.

In business, one of the challenges is making sure that your product is the easiest to experience and to sell.

I will give you another example. I buy a lot of consumer electronics. When I have a good idea of what I want, or if it's big and I don't want to have to drag it from the store, I buy through Amazon, as I just mentioned.

Other times I like to shop and kill time and see what's happening in the consumer electronics world. Two of the places I shop will let me take the product right to the checkout. That's easy. Another that I *used* to shop at made me tell a clerk what I wanted, who in turn went to the inventory room. I then had to go to the sales line where they would meet me with the merchandise. Two lines. One or both was usually more than a few people deep. I don't go back there anymore. It might have been easier for them, but it was slow and painful for me.

Moral of the story: Make your product easier to buy than your competition, or you will find your customers buying from them, not you.

Which brings me back to George Gilder and a topic I think will be fascinating to watch play out.

George and others seem to think that unlimited choice is the holy grail of TV. It's not.

The reason it's not is that it's too much work to page through an unlimited number of options. It's too much work to have to think of what it is we might like to watch. We are afraid we might miss something that we really did want to watch. Put another way, it's way too hard to shop for shows in a store where the aisles are endless. It's stressful and a lot of work. Which is exactly why when we channel surf, or when we surf the net, we all end up surfing the same 10, 15, 20 channels/sites over and over again. It's the path of least resistance.

It's also why websites do anything they can to game the system on search engines to get top ranking. They know that no one is going to page through the thousands of results the search returned. Users will pick from the first page or they will pick one of the sponsored ads long before they choose to browse through even a couple pages.

So when Gilder thinks we will only watch exactly what we want to watch, he is dead wrong, because we don't know what we want to watch as often as, if not more often than, we do know.

When we get to a point that there are thousands of on-demand TV choices, we won't approach TV programming guides like we do a search engine, looking for a specific target. That's too much work. The smart on-demand providers will present their programming guides more like Amazon.com or Netflix.com, both of which do a great job of "suggestive programming."

We will get a personalized page with options that it thinks we might like based on our previous viewing decisions. Then different categories of shows, within each we will see best rated, most viewed and newest added, along with "playlists" suggested by branded guides who make recommendations. All of these simple options will make it easy for us to make a choice with some level of confidence. We won't feel like we are missing something and we will know that if we don't like the show, we can quickly go back to a point that makes it easy to find another selection.

Aaron Spelling was exactly right when he said that TV is the best alternative to boredom. Future providers of on-demand content will hopefully remember this when devising their user interfaces, and every business should remember it as well.

Everyone follows the path of least resistance.

NEED A JOB?

No, I'm not hiring.

I do get hundreds of résumés and emails asking me for advice in finding a job. Most common are those from people who want a job in sports, and they want to know the best way to get there.

Well, here you go.

I. DON'T MAJOR IN SPORTS MARKETING

In my honest opinion, every one of the Sports Marketing programs, or the derivatives thereof, are a HUGE waste of time and resources. It's the 2000s version of "Rocks for Jocks" or majoring in Phys Ed. Can't think of what you want to major in? Working in sports sounds like a blast ... so let's pick Sports Marketing.

I know that's not completely fair to everyone. That's

a broad generalization. But from this end, it sure seems that way.

Let me let all Sports Marketing majors in on a secret. There is nothing at all special or different about running, managing or working in a sports organization. It runs the exact same way as any company that sells widgets, service or entertainment of any kind.

If you really want to work for a sports organization, get as broad based a business education as you possibly can. Finance, accounting, sales, more sales, even more sales, management, etc. The better the understanding you have of our customers and how they work, the better value you will be able to provide to the sports organization. To repeat, it's more important to know how our customers' businesses operate than how the sports business operates.

What we do is easy.

2. IF YOU CAN SELL, YOU CAN GET A JOB –ANYWHERE, ANYTIME

When I was growing up I was told over and over again, if you can sell, you can always get a job. Of course, I was told that after a friend of my mom's told me when I was in high school, that I should also have a trade to fall back on. He tried to teach me how to lay carpet. My first, last and only experience was working for him and watching him shake his head and rip out what I had done…. But I digress.

I don't remember who told me that selling was a job for a lifetime, but they were right.

If you can sell, you can find a job in sports. I will take a high school dropout who is caring, involved and can sell over an MBA in sports management almost every time.

What makes a good salesperson?

Let me be clear that it's not the person who can talk someone into anything. It's not the hustler who is a smooth talker. The best salespeople are the ones who put themselves in their customer's shoes and provide a solution that makes the customer happy.

The best salesperson is the one the customer trusts and never has to question.

The best salesperson is the one who knows that with every cold call made, he is closer to helping someone.

The best salesperson is the one who takes immense satisfaction from the satisfaction her customer gets.

The best salesperson is the one who wakes up early every morning excited to come to the office, get on the phone and let people know exactly why he loves his product, job and clients.

Sound corny? It is. It's also very simple.

And it's the most important job in every company.

There has yet to be a successful company that has survived with zero sales.

So if selling is the most important job in a company, why do fewer and fewer people seem to be wanting the job?

Why aren't there many colleges offering majors in Salesmanship, rather than Sales and Marketing? Just pure, old-fashioned selling?

If you don't have a job, or don't have the job you want, get a job in sales. Every single person on this planet can learn to be a great salesperson. All you have to do is put in the effort and care about your company, your prospects and customers.

Once you excel at selling, getting a job in sports is easy. But then again, if you are good, I'm sure the company you work for is going to do everything they can to keep you.

TAKING NO FOR AN ANSWER AND OTHER BUSINESS MISTAKES

It always cracks me up when someone peppers me with a product/service/idea and hits me with the refrain: "I won't take no for an answer," or, even better, "Would you take no for an answer?" Let me answer that question for you right now.

Hell, yes, I take no for an answer. I try to sell good products and services and have ideas that I hope will be successful. If I am selling any of these to someone and they say no, I will always ask for their objections with something like, "Thank you for taking the time to listen/read. Would you mind sharing with me what you didn't like about the product or why you like the product you chose?" And if I have a good counter to their objection(s), I will let it fly and see what happens.

If they still respond negatively to my efforts, so be it. At some point, and that point should come quickly, you have to move on. If you have a good product/service/idea, there will be someone who will understand the value and will want the product. If you keep on pushing with someone who obviously does not want the product for whatever reason, you are making multiple mistakes:

1. You are wasting your and the prospect's time. Wasting your time means you are not selling to the next prospect. Always remember what I tell myself: "Every no gets me closer to a yes." You have to move on and start communicating with someone you know might buy your product rather than wasting more time with someone you already know won't buy your product/service/idea.

2. The more you push someone who has said no, the more likely you are to appear desperate, and that desperation impacts your brand as a salesperson and the brand of the product. Just because it worked for Bud Fox doesn't mean it will work for you. That was a movie.

3. It's a sign of fear and laziness. It takes work to find qualified prospects. It also takes courage to overcome the fear of not knowing what will happen next. It is very, very easy to send someone an email every day or even hour. That is what a lazy person is going to do: spend all of two seconds hitting the resend button. A smart,

focused and successful salesperson will gear up and do the homework necessary to find their next customer. That is a sign of confidence.

If you believe deeply in what you do, it is going to be fun and exciting to find your next customer and show off how amazing your products/service/idea is. If the last person didn't get it, that's his or her problem. Not yours.

That is what successful businesspeople do. What do you do?

LIVING IN A TENSE ECONOMY, AKA SOMETIMES YOU HAVE TO SAY "WTF!"

This is the year of WTF. In fact, it could be said that this is the decade of WTF. Yep, What the F#@%!

It doesn't matter what got you to the point of saying it. Maybe you got fired or laid off. Maybe your company went out of business. Maybe you quit because you couldn't take it any longer. Maybe you are just graduating from school and the prospect of living at home is far worse than cramming into a beater house or apartment you call "The Hotel" with twelve other roommates. Whatever the reason, the question is: How do you turn this time into the start of something good?

I'm here to give you your WTF To-Do List.

I. RECOGNIZE THAT IT'S OKAY TO LIVE LIKE A STUDENT

It doesn't matter where you live. It doesn't matter how you live. It doesn't matter what kind of car you drive. It doesn't matter what kind of clothes you wear. It doesn't matter. Your biggest enemies are your bills. The more you owe, the more you stress. The more you stress over bills, the more difficult it is to focus on your goals. More importantly, if you set your monthly income requirements too high, you eliminate a significant number of opportunities. The cheaper you can live, the greater your options. Remember that.

2. TAKE LOTS OF CHANCES

If you are living cheaply and ready to find out where your future lies, now is the time to try anything. WTF-time means fighting through your fears to take a job in a new industry. It means trying different things to find out what it is you love to do. There will be no such thing as too many jobs. In this type of economy getting a job is tough if not often impossible, so you are going to have bust ass to create opportunities for yourself.

Creating opportunities means looking where others are not. Look outside of where all your friends are looking. Make a list of jobs and businesses that are beyond the norm. I know you want to follow your passions and get a job in sports, movies, TV, shooting video for Girls Gone Wild, and other things your friends would love. But why fight the crowds? Go where people are not.

Just like you never thought you would fall in love again after your first heartbreak, you will find another industry or job that you love as much. Move down your list to other things. Then get ready to work. Hard.

In this kind of economy, it really is a numbers game. You are going to have to keep on applying for anything and everything that opens a door you want to walk through. You can never slow down. It's hard work finding a job! If you have bills you have to pay, and it means taking a night job in order to keep looking for the day job or to keep a job you want, do it. Be a waiter, a night janitor, wash clothes, sell vacuum cleaners door-to-door—whatever you need to do, all the while reminding yourself that it opens the door to your future.

Then, when you do find a job, remind yourself that you are winging it. Everyone always sees the bright side of the job they just took. You have to. The new job you just scored that you thought would be amazing, will be amazing. Most likely it will be amazing for about three months. Then you will realize it's not so amazing and you will need to find something else that's amazing. That's okay. You don't have to be right every time. You just have to be right one time. Finding the right job is a lot like dating. It's hard until you start, then when you start, it's great until it's not. Then it's frustrating as hell until you get it right. But when you do, it all comes together.

3. FIGURE OUT IF YOU ARE IN THE RIGHT JOB

It's really easy to know if you are in the right job. If it matters how much you get paid, you are not in a job you really love. I'm not saying that you shouldn't want to make more money. I'm not saying that you shouldn't bust your ass to make as much money as possible. That's not the issue. The issue is whether or not you truly love your job. If you love what you do so much that you are willing to continue to live like a student in order to be able to stay in the job, you have found your calling.

4. FIGURE OUT HOW TO BE THE BEST

Once you have found out what you love to do, there is only one goal: to be the best in the world at it. It doesn't matter if you are a filing clerk, an athlete, an accountant or a bartender. All that matters is that you do whatever you can to be the best. Of course, "the best" is a relative term. The one person whom you should never believe when it comes to evaluating your abilities? You. The very worst judge of your abilities is you. Self-evaluation is never successful. When you are the best at something, the demand for your services will grow. People want to hire the best. They want to be associated with the best. In 2012, in this economy, so many people switch jobs and industries, and it's much easier to stay connected via social networks and other digital means, which means that people who need you can and will find you. So rather than trying to convince people you are the best, let the quality of your work do the talking.

5. START THE DAY MOTIVATED WITH A POSITIVE ATTITUDE

You are going to screw up. We all do. I can't tell you how many times I did and continue to. It happens too often. But no matter what happens, every morning, the minute after you wipe away the crust from your eyes, remind yourself that you are going to enjoy every minute of the day.

You are going to enjoy the twenty interviews you have. You are going to enjoy waiting in the heat for your roommate to pick you up afterward. You are going to enjoy realizing how frayed your collar has become and how sick you are of your one, lonesome tie. You are going to enjoy all the bullshit you have to deal with as you chase your goals and dreams, because you want to remember them all. Each and every experience will serve as motivation and provide great memories when you finally make it all happen.

It's your choice. What are you going to do?

WHY YOU SHOULD NEVER LISTEN TO YOUR CUSTOMERS

A great quote from technology luminary Alan Kay that every entrepreneur needs to remember: **"The best way to predict the future is to invent it."**

I'm working with a company that at one point had a product that was not only best in its class, but also technically far ahead of its competition. It created a better way of offering its service, and customers loved it and paid for it. Then it made a fatal mistake. It asked its customers what features they wanted to see in the product, and they delivered on those features. Unfortunately for this company, its competitors didn't ask customers what they wanted. Instead, they had a vision of ways that business could be done differently and, as a result, better. Customers didn't really see the value or need until they saw the new product. When they tried it, they loved it.

So what did "my" company do when it saw what its competitor had done? It repeated its mistake and once again asked its customers what they wanted in the product. Of course the customer responded with the features that they now loved from the other product.

The company didn't improve their competitive positioning. It put itself in a revolving door of trying to respond to customer requests. To make matters worse, resources and brainpower that could be applied to "inventing the future" were instead being used to catch up with features that locked the company into the past.

Entrepreneurs always need to be reminded that it's not the job of their customers to know what they don't. In other words, your customers have a tough enough time doing their jobs. They don't spend time trying to reinvent their industries or how their jobs are performed. Sure, every now and then you come across an exception. But you can't bet the company on your finding that person among your customers.

Instead, part of every entrepreneur's job is to invent the future. I also call it "kicking your own ass." Someone is out there looking to put you out of business. Someone is out there who thinks they have a better idea than you have. A better solution than you have. A better or more efficient product than you have. If there is someone out there who can "kick your ass" by doing it better, it's part of your job as the owner of the company to stay ahead of them and "kick your own ass" before someone else does.

Your customers can tell you the things that are broken

and how they want to be made happy. Listen to them. Make them happy. But don't rely on them to create the future road map for your product or service. That's your job.

TWELVE CUBAN RULES FOR STARTUPS

Anyone who has started a company has his own rules and guidelines, so I thought I would add to the memo with my own. My "rules" below aren't just for those founding the companies, but for those who are considering going to work for them, as well.

1. Don't start a company unless it's an obsession and something you love.

2. If you have an exit strategy, it's not an obsession.

3. Hire people who you think will love working there.

4. Sales Cure All. Know how your company will make money and how you will actually make sales.

5. Know your core competencies and focus on being great at them. Pay up for people in your core competencies. Get the best. Outside the core competencies, hire people that fit your culture but are cheap.

6. An espresso machine? Are you kidding me? Shoot yourself before you spend money on an espresso machine. Coffee is for closers. Sodas are free. Lunch is a chance to get out of the office and talk. There are 24 hours in a day, and if people like their jobs, they will find ways to use as much of it as possible to do their jobs.

7. No offices. Open offices keep everyone in tune with what is going on and keep the energy up. If an employee is about privacy, show them how to use the lock on the john. There is nothing private in a startup. This is also a good way to keep from hiring execs who cannot operate successfully in a startup. My biggest fear was always hiring someone who wanted to build an empire. If the person demands to fly first class or to bring over a personal secretary, run away. If an exec won't go on sales calls, run away. They are empire builders and will pollute your company.

8. As far as technology, go with what you know. That is always the cheapest way. If you know Apple, use it. If

you know Vista ... ask yourself why, then use it. It's a startup, there are just a few employees. Let people use what they know.

9. Keep the organization flat. If you have managers reporting to managers in a startup, you will fail. Once you get beyond startup, if you have managers reporting to managers, you will create politics.

10. NEVER EVER EVER buy swag. A sure sign of failure for a startup is when someone sends me logo-embroidered polo shirts. If your people are at shows and in public, it's okay to buy for your own folks, but if you really think someone is going to wear your YoBaby.com polo when they're out and about, you are mistaken and have no idea how to spend your money.

11. NEVER EVER EVER hire a PR firm. A PR firm will call or email people in the publications you already read, on the shows you already watch and at the websites you already surf. Those people publish their emails. Whenever you consume any information related to your field, get the email of the person publishing it and send them a message introducing yourself and the company. Their job is to find new stuff. They will welcome hearing from the founder instead of some PR flack. Once you establish communication with that person, make yourself available to answer their questions about the industry and be a source for them. If you are smart, they will use you.

12. Make the job fun for employees. Keep a pulse on the stress levels and accomplishments of your people and reward them. My first company, MicroSolutions, when we had a record sales month, or someone did something special, I would walk around handing out $100 bills to salespeople. At Broadcast.com and MicroSolutions, we had a company shot. The Kamikaze. We would take people to a bar every now and then and buy one or ten for everyone. At MicroSolutions, more often than not we had vendors cover the tab. Vendors always love a good party.

TWELVE CUBAN MANTRAS FOR SUCCESS

I. TIME IS MORE VALUABLE THAN MONEY

You have to learn how to use time wisely and be productive. How wisely you use your time will have far more impact on your life and success than any amount of money.

2. COMMIT RANDOM ACTS OF KINDNESS

Being successful entails being able to not only get along with people, but also to give something back. No one gets to the top on their own, and I believe we all should be able to make those around us smile.

3. NO BALLS, NO BABIES

This is something a blackjack dealer once told me when I asked him if I should hit or stick. It is also my favorite line and probably the thing I tell myself the most. Once you are prepared and you think you have every angle of preparation covered, *you have to go for it.* No balls, no babies.

4. WORK HARD, PLAY HARD

I went seven years without a vacation, but I sure managed to have fun. You have to find ways to blow off steam so you don't blow a gasket.

5. DON'T LET FEAR BE A ROADBLOCK

You can use fear as a roadblock or as motivation. There is always going to be someone who is competing with you, and sometimes they are going to win. Rather than not doing something for fear of losing, take on the challenge. If you fail, get back up and go for it again. I have been fired from more jobs than most people have had! In the search for success, you can fail any number of times, but you only have to get it right one time.

6. EXPECT THE UNEXPECTED, AND ALWAYS BE READY

You don't wake up in the morning with someone telling you that everyone is going to be selling lemonade so whoever sells the most wins. It's the exact opposite. Life is unpredictable.

You never know when a window of opportunity will open or close. You have to realize this and always know that the game is on. Whatever you are striving to achieve isn't waiting in one static place for you to find it. It's the opposite. **Everyone** has inside of them what it takes to be successful. You just have to be ready to unleash it when the opportunity presents itself.

7. IT'S OKAY TO YELL AND BE YELLED AT

One of the rules I have is that I don't mind if people raise their voice or even yell a little bit. At MicroSolutions, my partner Martin and I would have some knock-down drag-outs. They were always short bursts. They didn't happen a lot. When they did, I knew and he knew that this was an issue we were both passionate about.

As my businesses grew, it happened less often because people deferred to me more often. I hated that. If someone believed strongly enough in something and I was being passionate about something, I wanted them to match my level of passion.

So I told people that if they thought it was the only way to get through to me, go for it! This may not work for you in corporate America, but anyone in a family business or in a private business of any size with a partner or two knows exactly what I am talking about!

8. EVERYONE GETS DOWN: THE KEY IS HOW SOON YOU GET BACK UP

I can't count how many times I have gotten up in the morning dreading the day. I wasn't motivated. I was tired. I just wanted to crawl back in bed. Other times, I had lost a deal, we had lost a game, something wasn't working. I just wanted to crawl under a rock and disappear.

EVERYONE goes through those moments. The key is how you fight through them.

The people who will be truly successful are those that fight through the quickest and come back stronger and smarter.

9. IT'S NOT WHETHER THE GLASS IS HALF EMPTY OR HALF FULL, IT'S WHO IS POURING THE WATER

This is one of my favorites. The key in business and success at any endeavor is doing your best to control your destiny. You can't always do it, but you have to take every opportunity you can to be as prepared as—and ahead of—the competition as you possibly can be. Take the lead, and you can control your own destiny.

10. IT'S NOT IN THE DREAMING, IT'S IN THE DOING

Everyone has it in them to be successful. EVERYONE. Most people only dream about what they do if they were successful, or how they might get there. Anyone can dream. Anyone and everyone has ideas about how they might be successful. It doesn't matter if your definition of success is being a great parent, being an athlete, a business person, whatever.

When I catch myself daydreaming about how I'm going to do this or that, I always try to wake up and ask myself just how I'm going to get from where I am to where I want to be. What EXACTLY is it going to take to DO it, rather than dream about it.

II. PIGS GET FAT, HOGS GET SLAUGHTERED

This is one I got from my partner Todd Wagner. He is right on. Sometimes you have to go for the jugular, but more often than not, the biggest mistake people make is getting too greedy.

Every good deal has a win-win solution. There is nothing I hate more than someone who tries to squeeze every last penny out of the deal. Who often raises the aggravation level to the point where it's not worth doing the deal. Which also raises the dislike level to the point where even if a deal gets done, you look for ways to never do business with that person or company again.

Business happens over years and years. Value is measured in the total upside of a business relationship, not by how much you squeezed out in any one deal.

12. YOU ONLY HAVE TO BE RIGHT ONCE

As I've said, I have been fired from more jobs than most

people have had. Some jobs I have had were so bad, the only way I could justify them to myself was that I was getting paid to learn (as opposed to paying to go to school).

I have started a stupid business that was doomed to fail (selling powdered milk). I have dated more girls than I wanted to. The beauty of success, whether it's finding the girl of your dreams, the right job or financial success, is that it doesn't matter how many times you have failed, you only have to be right once.

No one keeps score. There are so many ways that each of us can find happiness and success in our endeavors, that it never really matters how many times you fail. You only have to be right once.

These are some of the things I use to guide myself in different situations. Maybe they apply to your situation, maybe they don't. That's up to you to decide.